Endorsements fo

"The Christmas s
some, great sorrow. Which is why I'm thankful for the work of Abby Ball, and the deep tenderness she leads with in her devotional, "Contemplating Christmas." With compassion and wisdom, Abby reminds us that Emmanuel, God With us, meets us precisely where we are; both in our hope and our pain. Abby beautifully beckons us to remember that our sacred work is not to deny the reality of our humanity as we walk through Christmas, but instead, to recall that the One who created us comes near as we face whatever our lives hold. I am so grateful for this gorgeous resource."

Aundi Kolber, MA, LPC, Therapist and Author of *Try Softer* and *Strong like Water*

"Abby has a beautiful, poetic style of writing that draws the reader in immediately. She has created a refreshingly different Advent devotional that is honest about the struggles and difficulties of life, but also invites us to push past the consumerism and cultural expectations of the season to draw closer to Jesus - even in the midst of our questions and hurting. Her reflection questions are insightful, helping the reader to really think and apply what they have been reading about, and the breath prayers are wonderful, easy takeaways to use throughout the day. This is a rich resource that offers a gentle yet powerful accompaniment to Advent."

Claire Musters, author, speaker, editor and host of the Woman Alive book club.

"Advent provides a necessary alternative to the ways the Christmas season has become a time of consumption and excess. What Abby Ball offers in her new Advent Devotional "Contemplating Christmas" is just what we need: a beautiful reiteration of the simple and essential invitation to watch and wait. Inhale: There is so much darkness. Exhale: Jesus is coming."

Christiana Peterson, author of *Mystics & Misfits* and *Awakened by Death*.

"Through meaningful reflection and thoughtful questions—delivered by caring hands—Abby Ball leads us heart-first into the season of Advent. If melancholy or painful memories have ever sat gift-wrapped beneath your Christmas tree, you will find in these pages an invitation to hold your story with honesty and grace and offer it all to the Saviour."
Jonathan Puddle, pastor and author of *You Are Enough: Learning to Love Yourself the Way God Loves You* **and** *Mornings with God: Daily Bible Devotional for Men*

"Christmas can be a time when life gets overwhelming as the world piles more and more ideals of perfection and happiness on us. Abby Ball's new Advent devotional is a warm and inviting counterbalance to these unsettling messages. It's a place to sit down in the silence and to find God there with us when our lives are less than perfect. Abby's words are lyrical and beautiful, and welcome us into a place of authenticity and vulnerability, where we can admit to the difficulties of life while finding hope in this great and enduring story of love come down. Contemplating Christmas is a lavish feast, a gentle rest and an enticing journey to joy, and it will soothe your weary places this Advent season."
Liz Carter, author of *Catching Contentment* **and the upcoming** *Valuable*

"Abby Ball is a writer of rare fluency and clarity. She is a voice of authenticity in a world which can present itself as unattainably glossy and perfect at times. Her devotional for the Advent season is a welcome addition to a crowded marketplace. "Contemplating Christmas" has been written for those for whom the glitter, sparkle and relentless cheeriness of the season can be just too much. Gentle, reflective and insightful, this is a place where readers can come and be reminded of the true spirit of Christmas, the breathless wait for the Christ Child, the darkness before the revelation of the radiance of His love."
Ruth Leigh, author of the *Isabella M Smugge* **series.**

CONTEMPLATING CHRISTMAS

An Advent Devotional for Finding Hope in the Dark

BY ABBY BALL

For Tim

CONTENTS

The Invitation of Advent

Christmas is here again, dressed in all its traditional finery. We're knee-deep in wrapping paper, fairy lights, gift lists and mince pies. We've been watching holiday adverts and Hallmark movies for months and Andy Williams still thinks it's the most wonderful time of the year. But despite the glitter and sparkle we like to throw all over it, Christmas does not always bring unbridled joy. If you're struggling to make ends meet, the coercive consumerism of endless advertising can feel unbearably shaming. If you've lost someone dear to you, Christmas celebrations can feel jarring as you're overwhelmed by yet another wave of grief. If you live with a broken dream, a chronic illness or a difficult family situation, Christmas can be a painful reminder of all the ways in which life hasn't worked out like you hoped it would.

So here's what I want to know: What might Christmas have to offer us when we're hurting or in despair? Does the Christmas story still have something to say to us when the party is over and we've long-since stopped believing in Santa Claus? How do we dig underneath the thick layer of cultural expectations for Christmas and find the presence of God?

The season of Advent holds space for such questions. In the northern hemisphere, Advent falls during the darkest month, when the days are short, the daylight is all too fleeting and hope seems foolish and naïve. But Advent invites us to a hope that makes room for our despair, and still has the capacity to wait and watch through the night in anticipation of what God might yet do. In Advent, we remember that Jesus was born into the world, while we also long for the ways he might come again. This season invites us to sit with our unmet desires and our waiting, as well as our joy and celebration. It reminds us that God is present in the middle of our chaos, uncertainty and pain as well as our moments of victory and triumph. Advent invites us to lean again into the mystery and majesty of God become human and makes space for us to imagine what miracles might be possible in our lives, and the lives of those around us.

To help us explore Advent, this book is structured around four themes: hope, peace, joy and love. Hope, that we might know God is still at work, even when we can't see it. Peace, that we might find stillness for our souls and justice for our world. Joy, that we might find delight to sustain us in the midst of suffering. And love, that we might come to know the fullness of our identity as beloved children of God.

Each day, you'll find a meditation, some questions to support your own reflection and a breath prayer – two simple phrases to repeat as you inhale and exhale – your own breath reminding you of the nearness of God.

So as we begin our Advent journey together, this is my prayer for you:

May the God of hope fill you with all joy and peace
as you trust in him,
So that you may overflow with hope
by the power of the Holy Spirit.

Romans 15:13

And may you find Immanuel, God with us, very close to you this Christmas.

WEEK 1

Hope

DAY 1

Be Still

Psalm 46

God is our refuge and strength,
an ever-present help in trouble.
Therefore we will not fear, though the earth give way
and the mountains fall into the heart of the sea,
though its waters roar and foam
and the mountains quake with their surging...

"Be still, and know that I am God;
I will be exalted among the nations,
I will be exalted in the earth."

The LORD Almighty is with us;
the God of Jacob is our fortress.

The beginning of Advent often finds us frantic and frazzled as the days between now and Christmas threaten to rush by in a blur of activity. We can find ourselves contending with the expectation to be perfect and the pressure to perform as we make our plans to celebrate. It's supposed to be a magical time of year, and yet nothing that happens at Christmas comes about by magic. Gifts must be chosen and wrapped, food needs to be bought and cooked, the house has to be cleaned and decorated. And everything is meant to be just right, for everyone. It's a lot of work when the days are short and our lives are busy.

But Advent offers us an invitation to press pause on the hustle of all our preparations. It's a season that invites us to slow down, savour the moment and turn our hearts towards holy anticipation. As we count down the days until Christmas with our candles and calendars, we're invited to remember that what we're really counting down to is not the perfect family celebration: rather, we are looking forward to Jesus being born into the world anew.

We tell the nativity story every year, not because we can't remember it, but to remind ourselves that we are God's people and that this is our story. It's the story of Jesus' birth and the birthplace of all our hope. It's the story of the incarnation: God coming to earth in all the vulnerability and mess of a human birth, to experience life as a human being so he could come and be with us, right where we are.

The word 'advent' is from the Latin, *adventus*, which translates as 'coming.' So when you hear the Christmas stories again this Advent, let them spark hope in you. The God who came as a baby two thousand years ago, can still come to you, in all the ways you need him to. Each time you open a calendar door, or light your Advent candle, let it become a ritual that offers you a moment to pause. In that small pause, take a breath, remember to treat yourself with kindness and still your soul long enough to hear the Spirit's whisper: "Relax, everything's going to be all right; rest, everything's coming together; open your hearts, love is on the way!" (Jude 2 **The Message**)

Reflection

What keeps you the most busy at this time of year?

How does the thought of slowing down and finding some stillness make you feel?

Breath prayer

Inhale: I will be still

Exhale: And know you are God.

DAY 2

Acknowledge the Dark

Luke 1:5-7

In the days of Herod, king of Judea, there was a priest named Zechariah, of the division of Abijah. And he had a wife from the daughters of Aaron, and her name was Elizabeth. And they were both righteous before God, walking blamelessly in all the commandments and statutes of the Lord. But they had no children because Elizabeth was barren, and both were advanced in years.

Matthew 2:16-18

When Herod realised he had been outwitted by the Magi, he was furious, and he gave orders to kill all the boys in Bethlehem and its vicinity who were 2 years old and under, in accordance with the time he had learned from the Magi. Then what was said through the prophet Jeremiah was fulfilled:

> *"A voice is heard in Ramah,*
> *weeping and great mourning,*
> *Rachel weeping for her children*
> *and refusing to be comforted,*
> *because they are no more."*

Our journey to Bethlehem is a familiar one. Since childhood we've been travelling the same well-worn routes to find the baby in the manger. We know the traditions we'll participate in, the stories we'll tell, the food we'll eat. We know which markers to look out for along the way: carols, Christmas cards, a school nativity play. We know it should all be bathed in the soft glow of twinkling fairy lights to make it feel merry and bright.

But what if it doesn't feel like that?

What if our familiar routes look more like family dysfunction that plays out the same way every year? What if the paths we're travelling down are well-worn grooves of disappointment and despair? What if we're walking the same old road of disability, loneliness or grief?

I find it comforting that the Christmas stories make room for sorrow, as well as joy. Elizabeth suffered through infertility. Joseph thought his fiancée had cheated on him. The toddlers of Bethlehem were murdered by an evil tyrant. These parts of the narrative are not missed out or glossed over. They are right there in the mix with all the angelic songs and celebrations. We'll get to joy later in our journey, but first, I want to you to know that in Advent, there is room for your sorrow as well as your celebration, your despair as well as your joy.

Authentic hope doesn't speak in platitudes or offer easy answers. It doesn't promise that everything will work out the way you want it to. Instead, it acknowledges the truth that life is sometimes difficult, disappointing and painful. It looks reality in the face and still makes room for what might yet be possible. I don't know what feels dark for you right now, but God does. And if you can't hold onto hope right now, may you find that hope is holding onto you.

Reflection

Which parts of this season feel difficult for you?

How does it feel to think of God being present with you in the darkness?

Breath prayer

Inhale: Lord, there is so much darkness.

Exhale: You are here with me.

DAY 3

Hold Space

Luke 1:11-15

Then an angel of the Lord appeared to him, standing at the right side of the altar of incense. When Zechariah saw him, he was startled and was gripped with fear. But the angel said to him: "Do not be afraid, Zechariah; your prayer has been heard. Your wife Elizabeth will bear you a son, and you are to call him John. He will be a joy and delight to you, and many will rejoice because of his birth, for he will be great in the sight of the Lord."

Over four hundred years separate the Old Testament and the New Testament. This was liminal space – that in-between time when God's prophets had finished speaking, but God's next words had not yet been spoken. That's a lot of years to wait in the face of God's silence. During this time God's people had to hold space for his promise. They had to hold space for their own questions, doubts and disillusionment. They held on with a gritty, stubborn hope that was more like gravel under their knees than a comfort blanket round their shoulders.

When the word of the Lord finally came, it was to introduce another period of waiting – the time it would take for John to the Baptist to grow in his mother's womb until he could be safely delivered. For Zechariah and Elizabeth, this was liminal space: their childless years were over, but they were still waiting for the birth of their son. The promised had been made but not yet fulfilled.

We can end up 'betwixt and between' for all sort of reasons. Grief will do that for you. So will moving to a new place, family or friendship changes. I don't know what your 'in-between' looks like right now, but you do, and so does God. However we get there, liminal space can be disconcerting and painful. We feel the anxiety of the uncertain and the unknown. We're compelled to learn patience and to let go of all the things we can't control.

But Advent reminds us that liminal space is also holy ground. As we wait for Jesus, who was born, and is still yet to come into the world, we take hope knowing this time is also a threshold: an open door where something new might emerge. If we're wise enough to sit with the discomfort, the in-between times can become places of vital transformation. Liminality might feel like death, but we're actually experiencing the birth pains of new life. We've arrived at this place precisely because we're NOT stuck and stagnant but growing and alive. So we struggle and wait and work with the process as the Holy Spirit recreates us from the inside.

As we hold space for the uncomfortable and the unknown, we find that God has stayed right there with us. Grace is still holding us, and God's comfort and care find us in ways we never thought to ask for or imagine. And we hold onto the certain hope that something beautiful is waiting for us on the other side.

Reflection

Where in your life feels like liminal space, or an 'in-between' time right now?

How does it feel to think of that place as a threshold, where something new and beautiful might emerge?

Breath Prayer

Inhale: I hold space for the unknown

Exhale: Help me find hope for new life.

DAY 4

Find Light

Genesis 1:5

In the beginning, God created the heavens and the earth. Now the earth was formless and empty, darkness was over the surface of the deep, and the Spirit of God was hovering over the waters.

And God said "Let there be light," and there was light. God saw that the light was good, and he separated the light from the darkness God called the light "day," and the darkness he called "night." And there was evening, and there was morning – the first day.

John 1:1-5

In the beginning was the Word, and the Word was with God, and the Word was God. He was with God in the beginning. Through him all things were made; without him nothing was made that has been made. In him was life, and that life was the light of all mankind. The light shines in the darkness, and the darkness has not overcome it.

At this time of year, in the northern hemisphere at least, the earth turns towards darkness. By the time we reach Advent, our hours of daylight have diminished and our nights are long. Night time brings with it a sharpened sense of our own vulnerability. Fears we can easily dismiss during the day keep us awake at night. What is familiar in the daylight becomes strange and disorienting in the dark. St John of the Cross coined the phrase 'the dark night of the soul,' to describe seasons when the darkness we feel becomes so consuming we lose sight of God.

But though darkness can be so hard on body and soul, God does not choose to banish it. Right from the beginning of creation, he sets up a beautiful interplay between dark and light, knowing we need the rhythm of both. We see by the daylight but we can't sleep without the dark. We revel in the beauty of summer, but need winter so the earth can rest. Dawn emerges from night, seeds germinate underground, babies are conceived in the secrecy of their mother's womb. So much that is new begins in the hiddenness and obscurity of the dark.

Advent offers us an invitation to lean into the darkness and embrace the holy mystery of what is unseen. It's a season to keep company with all our longing and all our hope. We don't know what's happening under the ground and we often can't see what's going on beneath the surface of our own lives. But God is at work there. So we watch and wait as the Spirit hovers over the darkness, to see what she will bring to life.

I think about the two women who went into the darkness of the tomb to anoint Jesus' body with spices. They came expecting only death and grief, but what they found instead was resurrection: the restoration of all their hope, right in the very place of their deepest despair.

So perhaps this Advent we can light our candles and string up our fairy lights, not to dispel the darkness, but to decorate it. Perhaps we can find hope in the glimmer and sparkle around us, tangible reminders that the light shines in the darkness and the darkness has not overcome it.

Reflection

What are you hoping and longing for this Advent?

How might you choose to 'decorate the dark?'

Breath Prayer

Inhale: I can't see what's going on.

Exhale: I will wait and watch for you.

DAY 5

Take Heart

Lamentations 3:22-24

Because of the Lord's great love
we are not consumed,
for his compassions never fail.
They are new every morning;
great is your faithfulness.
I say to myself, "The Lord is my portion;
therefore I will wait for him."

Song of Songs 2:10-13

My beloved spoke and said to me,
"Arise, my darling,
my beautiful one, come with me.
See! The winter is past;
the rains are over and gone.
Flowers appear on the earth;
the season of singing has come…"

Winter seasons are about endurance and survival as the landscape becomes stark and inhospitable. Resources are scarce and there are no visible signs of life. Trees are stripped bare, the earth is devoid of colour and the air is bitter. Grey skies overhead and damp paths underfoot make everything seem dreary and hopeless. Winter's chill settles deep into your bones, no matter how many layers you wear. Just putting one foot in front of the other seems to take all the energy you can muster.

But under the surface of the earth, something essential is happening. Trees are replenishing their nutrients from deep below the ground. Seeds are bedding down and establishing their roots. Animals are resting in preparation for the coming activities of spring. The old is being cleared away, ready for new life to emerge.

Perhaps in our own winter seasons we can learn from the natural environment. Perhaps it's okay to have seasons that don't appear to be productive. Perhaps it's okay to let some things lie fallow for a while. Maybe what we most need is rest and replenishment. In winter, we reach for hearty, nourishing food to fill our stomachs. Maybe we can reach for something hearty and nourishing to fill our souls, too.

Of course, we know that winter does not last forever. Spring returns to us faithfully each year. The days will gradually lengthen and the earth will slowly return to warmth. Crocuses and daffodils will bring back colour as they emerge from beneath the ground. Birds will sing to us again, reminding us that all is not lost and that hope is on the way. While we wait for spring to arrive, it helps to notice the gifts of this season. That one ray of sunshine, the beauty of a frosty morning, cosy blankets, hot drinks, warm-hearted friends. In choosing to notice theses simple pleasures, we send out little shoots into the soil, rooting and establishing ourselves into the goodness of God. We take heart, reminding ourselves that even here in the depths of winter, God's mercies are still new every morning.

Reflection

What small mercies might you notice today?

What might be nourishing for your soul in this season?

Breath prayer

Inhale: Even in winter times

Exhale: Help me find goodness.

DAY 6

Wonderful Counsellor

Isaiah 9:6-7

For to us a child is born,
to us a son is given,
and the government will be on his shoulders.
And he will be called
Wonderful Counsellor, Mighty God,
Everlasting Father, Prince of Peace.
Of the greatness of his government and peace
there will be no end.
He will reign on David's throne
and over his kingdom,
establishing and upholding it
with justice and righteousness
from that time on and forever.
The zeal of the LORD Almighty
will accomplish this.

Advent can be a challenging season. As we wait for Christmas, everything else that we are waiting for is brought to the surface. We are more aware than ever of living in the tension between the already but not yet of God's kingdom. We know that Jesus has already come, but we are fully awake to all the ways we still need him to come, both personally and in our world. We've seen the evidence of God's kindness in our own lives and yet we still live with unresolved heartache and unanswered questions. We've celebrated as we've seen unjust structures dismantled and yet we cry out in anger at the systems still crushing the life out of the poor and the marginalised. We've known beauty, peace and breakthrough and yet remain in desperate need of God's compassion, justice and mercy to come again.

The Wonderful Counsellor, in his infinite wisdom, is able to take all the disparate pieces of our lives and weave them into something new. He makes room for all that life brings to us: the sorrow, the joy, the messy, the broken, the mundane, the sublime, the ridiculous and everything in between. Nothing we experience is left outside of the loving hands of God. He is with us in it all.

So the invitation of Advent is hope. Hope reminds us that this is not the end of our story. Hope sings to us precisely *because* we don't know how things will work out. We don't yet see all the ways God will show up to heal what's been broken, redeem what's been lost and bring life to all that we thought was dead. We don't know how it will all unfold, but we do know that God is faithful to his promises. We hold onto his goodness even while we lament in our waiting. We trust his promise that his government and his peace will not fail to increase. We wait and we watch knowing that the Wonderful Counsellor holds all things together, holds us close, and will make everything beautiful in its time.

Reflection

Where have you experienced God's kindness? Where are you still waiting for breakthrough?

How does hope feel for you right now? Vulnerable? Helpful? Frustrating? Something else?

Breath Prayer

Inhale: Wonderful Counsellor

Exhale: My hope is in you.

WEEK 2

Peace

DAY 7

Fear Not

Luke 1:26-38

In the sixth month of Elizabeth's pregnancy, God sent the angel Gabriel to Nazareth, a town in Galilee, to a virgin pledged to be married to a man named Joseph, a descendant of David. The virgin's name was Mary. The angel went to her and said, "Greetings, you who are highly favoured! The Lord is with you."

Mary was greatly troubled at his words and wondered what kind of greeting this might be. But the angel said to her, "Do not be afraid, Mary; you have found favour with God. You will conceive and give birth to a son, and you are to call him Jesus. He will be great and will be called the Son of the Most High. The Lord God will give him the throne of his father David, and he will reign over Jacob's descendants forever; his kingdom will never end."

"How will this be," Mary asked the angel, "since I am a virgin?"

The angel answered, "The Holy Spirit will come on you, and the power of the Most High will overshadow you. So the holy one to be born will be called the Son of God. Even Elizabeth your relative is going to have a child in her old age, and she who was said to be unable to conceive is in her sixth month. For no word from God will ever fail."

"I am the Lord's servant," Mary answered. "May your word to me be fulfilled." Then the angel left her.

We don't pay much attention to angels at other times of the year, but at Christmas, we're all in. From chubby-cheeked cherubs on Christmas cards, to school children in fairy wings and tinsel halos, we embrace them all. It's not surprising given the frequency of angelic appearances in the nativity story. They visit an old man working at his job, a bunch of shepherds minding their own business and a young woman named Mary. God's messengers don't wait for the perfect moment or the holiest recipient. They come, in the middle of the ordinary and mundane circumstances of life, to normal people who are going about their everyday business.

It's easy to read the words of today's text with some trepidation. Mary's world is about to get completely turned upside down: the birth of Jesus will bring great heartbreak and suffering, alongside great honour and joy. So the angel brings her words of comfort: *Do not be afraid, Mary, you have found favour with God.*

It sometimes feels like there is so much to fear. Fear of change, fear that everything will stay the same. Fear of what we know, fear of what we don't know. Fear of ourselves or our loved ones being hurt, fear of tragedies that touch the lives of people we'll never know. Fear of speaking out, fear of staying silent. Fear of people who feel strange to us, fear of what our neighbours might think. Underneath it all, what we're really asking is: *Can God be trusted? Is God good? Does he **know** me?*

Angels are scattered throughout the narrative of Jesus's birth to remind us that God is still at work in our world. Mary had legitimate reasons to be afraid and so do we. But the words that brought her peace can bring us peace too. *Don't be afraid, you are highly favoured, God has seen you, I'm bringing good news.* God has noticed our lives and heard our prayers. We are his beloved children and he *knows* us. Peace is a gift the Holy Spirit gives to us; peace when it would make more sense to panic. Peace in spite of what we know could go wrong. Peace when everything seems bleak and chaotic. Peace when we're expected to go to pieces and collapse. Let's meditate on the angel's words today: don't be afraid. And let's ask the Holy Spirit to bring us peace where we need it most.

Reflection

What are you most afraid of right now?

How might you bring that before God?

Breath Prayer

Inhale: I will fear no evil

Exhale: You are with me.

DAY 8

Embrace Silence

Luke 2:8-15

And there were shepherds living out in the fields nearby, keeping watch over their flocks at night. An angel of the Lord appeared to them, and the glory of the Lord shone around them, and they were terrified. But the angel said to them, "Do not be afraid. I bring you good news that will cause great joy for all the people. Today in the town of David a Saviour has been born to you; he is the Messiah, the Lord. This will be a sign to you: You will find a baby wrapped in cloths and lying in a manger."

Suddenly a great company of the heavenly host appeared with the angel, praising God and saying,

"Glory to God in the highest heaven, and on earth peace to those on whom his favour rests."

When the angels had left them and gone into heaven, the shepherds said to one another, "Let's go to Bethlehem and see this thing that has happened, which the Lord has told us about."

I often wonder what it sounded like when the angels sang together to announce the birth of Jesus: the melody, the harmonies, the texture, the blend of voices. I imagine a moving, uplifting sound, with a huge swell of emotion as the music soars to welcome the baby king. It must have been incredibly beautiful.

But I also wonder what it was like in the moments after the music had died away. I imagine a holy hush descending, the peace tangible in the still air. I imagine the shepherds pausing for a moment in awe, breathing it all in.

There's no doubt the carols and songs of this season are beautiful but there's a lot of other noise that clamours for our attention too. Relentless advertising, the constant chatter of social media, the pressing opinions of other people. Perhaps it would serve us well to push pause on it all and join the shepherds in a moment of silence.

When we make time to be silent, we often find it can be both holy *and* hard. Sometimes the peace and quiet is a sweet relief. And sometimes, in moments of silence the things we try to push away, numb or ignore come to the surface. Painful memories, unhealed wounds, self-criticism. Sometimes the loudest voices are the ones in our own head. It's no wonder we live with the constant background noise of Netflix, Spotify, social media, podcasts – anything to avoid feeling our own pain.

But if we don't deal with our pain it shows up in other ways. It shows up as insecurity, a bad attitude, hurtful comments. It gets expressed as isolation, anxiety and fear. Unacknowledged pain becomes toxic to us and those around us.

If we can find the courage to sit with silence, it gives us the opportunity to express our emotions before God, whose love and grace are wide enough to hold all our feelings. And as we continue to stay with the silence, we find that we can move through our emotions and get quiet for long enough to hear the still, small voice that calls us by name, calls us beloved and calls us home. It's a sure pathway to peace.

Reflection

How might silence be helpful for you? How might it be hard?

What support might you need as you process some of your feelings?

Breath prayer

Inhale: In this silence

Exhale: I rest in you.

DAY 9

Go Gently

Luke 2:1-7

In those days Caesar Augustus issued a decree that a census should be taken of the entire Roman world. (This was the first census that took place while Quirinius was governor of Syria.) And everyone went to their own town to register.

So Joseph also went up from the town of Nazareth in Galilee to Judea, to Bethlehem the town of David, because he belonged to the house and line of David. He went there to register with Mary, who was pledged to be married to him and was expecting a child. While they were there, the time came for the baby to be born, and she gave birth to her firstborn, a son. She wrapped him in cloths and placed him in a manger, because there was no guest room available for them.

We spend a lot of time during Advent marvelling at the God who came down to earth as a tiny baby. We try to wrap our minds around the mystery of the incarnation – how the God of the whole universe chose to squeeze himself into such a small package. As we reaffirm our belief that Jesus was both fully God and fully human, I have often found it easier to focus on his divinity, as though that makes his (and our) humanity more acceptable. But today's reading invites us to think about Jesus' and our own human nature in a different way.

Jesus began his life on earth just as we do, as a new-born baby. Just like all babies, he was completely helpless and vulnerable, totally dependent on the kindness and care of his parents to keep him safe and well. This story of God-become-man helps us to understand that being vulnerable and having needs isn't a sign of weakness, it's a sign of being a human person. The Son of God had the same needs we do: physical needs for food, shelter and rest. Emotional needs for love, comfort and safety, spiritual needs for meaning, purpose and relationship with God. It's hard to admit to our needs sometimes, but recognising our own needs and vulnerabilities is part of what it means to be fully human, part of what it means to be like Jesus.

Of course, Jesus didn't spend his whole life as a little baby and neither do we. Part of growing up and maturing is understanding that we are, on the whole, responsible for meeting our own needs.[i] So we take care of our bodies, we nurture healthy relationships, we ask for help when we need it. We do the work of learning and growing emotionally and spiritually as we discover all that it means to flourish as a human being.

So let's go gently with ourselves today. Let's remember that it's okay to have needs. Let's speak to ourselves kindly and with tenderness. Let's embrace the full extent of our humanity, including our vulnerabilities and weaknesses as well as our strengths, remembering that to honour our full humanity is to honour the God in whose image we have been created. And as we treat ourselves gently, let's treat those around us with gentleness too.

Reflection

What do you need today? How might you meet that need?

Who, in your world, would appreciate being treated with gentleness today?

Breath Prayer

Inhale: Just as you are fully human

Exhale: I embrace my own humanity.

DAY 10

Find Rest

Psalm 23

The Lord is my shepherd, I lack nothing.
He makes me lie down in green pastures,
he leads me beside quiet waters,
he refreshes my soul.
He guides me along the right paths
for his name's sake.

Even though I walk
through the darkest valley,
I will fear no evil,
for you are with me;
your rod and your staff,
they comfort me.

You prepare a table before me
in the presence of my enemies.
You anoint my head with oil;
my cup overflows.
Surely your goodness and love will follow me
all the days of my life,
and I will dwell in the house of the Lord
forever.

Matthew 11:28-30

"Come to me, all you who are weary and burdened, and I will give you rest. Take my yoke upon you and learn from me, for I am gentle and humble in heart, and you will find rest for your souls. For my yoke is easy and my burden is light."

We live in a culture that tells us the story of scarcity. We're sold the idea that Christmas will be okay if only our children have enough of the right kind of presents to open. It'll be okay if we keep everyone happy, fed and entertained. It'll be okay if we just work hard enough to make it all a success. Only there never seems to be enough to mitigate our anxieties and soothe our stress. So we work harder and harder, never having a moment to stop for long enough and question our culture's definition of what makes us valuable and successful. But our anxiety and stress are cues that something is wrong. Our bodies are letting us know we weren't made to live like this.

The good news is that Jesus offers us a way out. He gives us the opportunity to live in a different story, the story of enough. Our true identity is not in what we have, what we do or what other people think about us.[ii] Our true identity is in being the beloved child of God. As God's beloved children, we can be at peace, knowing we have everything we need to meet the challenges that come our way. We can let go our old ways of seeking love and affirmation and rest in the love of God that we never have to earn. When we are secure in God's love, there's nothing left to prove. We can rest from the need for more stuff, rest from the need to say 'yes' to everything, rest from the need for other people's approval. Taking time to physically rest is a radically counter-cultural way to live. It's a way to step off the hamster wheel of production and consumption and actively put our trust in Jesus.

So when we're tempted to buy just a few more things for Christmas, go at an even faster pace than usual, or worry about what others are thinking of us, let's consider when it might be time to say 'enough is enough.' May we learn to say *my identity is rooted in the love of the Good Shepherd and he is enough for me.*

Reflection

How might you be listening the story of scarcity?

How might your body be telling you to slow down and rest?

Breath prayer

Inhale: The Lord is my Shepherd

Exhale: I have everything I need.

DAY 11

Make Peace

Psalm 85:8-13

I will listen to what God the LORD says;
he promises peace to his people, his faithful servants—
but let them not turn to folly.
Surely his salvation is near those who fear him,
that his glory may dwell in our land.

Love and faithfulness meet together;
righteousness and peace kiss each other.
Faithfulness springs forth from the earth,
and righteousness looks down from heaven.
The LORD will indeed give what is good,
and our land will yield its harvest.
Righteousness goes before him
and prepares the way for his steps.

Matthew 5:9

Blessed are the peacemakers,
for they will be called children of God.

When we think about the righteousness (or right living) that Psalm 85 describes, we often assume it means following a set of rules. If we're nice to others, don't steal or cheat and go to church on Sunday, then we will be at peace. But Jesus had a much more expansive vision for what it means to live well as one of God's people. He said that only two things were necessary: to love God with all that you are, and to love your neighbour as yourself (Matthew 22:34-40).

It sounds very simple, but this is much more challenging than following a set of rules. Following the way of Jesus means I have to think for myself. I have to consider what it might look like in practice to love God. I need to think about who my neighbour is and how I might love them well.

"But what's all this got to do with peace?" you might ask. It turns out – everything. When we make peace, we're not just avoiding conflicting and staying quiet so we don't rock the boat. That's not *making* peace, that's *keeping* the peace in order to maintain the status quo. But the trouble is, the status quo isn't working for many of our neighbours. It's not working for our female neighbours who can't walk down the street in safety and don't always have autonomy over their own bodies. It's not working for our black and brown neighbours who endure ongoing personal and systemic racism and police brutality. It's not working for our refugee neighbours, our neighbours who live in poverty or who suffer the effects of climate change.

If right living is to love our neighbours as ourselves, then loving our neighbours means speaking out about the injustices they face. This is a hard truth for someone like me who hates conflict. But the kind of peace Jesus offers isn't just a nice feeling for me personally, it's the opportunity for every single one of us to live in peace and safety so we can flourish.

This Advent, let's start making peace in specific ways where we are. Let's donate to a local foodbank, support a charity or email our representatives in government. Let's speak out next time we hear a sexist joke, or a racist comment. Let's educate ourselves about climate change or the causes of poverty. Let's be real peacemakers, as we more fully inhabit our identity as the children of God.

Reflection

How do you feel about the call to be a peacemaker, rather than a peacekeeper?

What's one small thing you could do to love a neighbour today?

Breath prayer

Inhale: You are our peacemaker.

Exhale: Teach me to make peace.

DAY 12

Mary's Song

Luke 1:45-55

And Mary said:

"My soul glorifies the Lord
and my spirit rejoices in God my Saviour,
for he has been mindful
of the humble state of his servant.
From now on all generations will call me blessed,
for the Mighty One has done great things for me—
holy is his name.
His mercy extends to those who fear him,
from generation to generation.
He has performed mighty deeds with his arm;
he has scattered those who are proud
in their inmost thoughts.
He has brought down rulers from their thrones
but has lifted up the humble.
He has filled the hungry with good things
but has sent the rich away empty.
He has helped his servant Israel,
remembering to be merciful
to Abraham and his descendants forever,
just as he promised our ancestors."

Have you ever noticed that people become a lot more charitable at Christmas? The train station in my home town hosts a Christmas Day lunch for the city's homeless population. A colleague raises funds so children living in poverty can have new toys. Santa hands out gifts to refugees living in a hostel. There are appeals to check in with elderly neighbours, or people who are far from home so they don't spend Christmas alone. We have a shared understanding that everyone should be invited to the celebration, everyone should be welcome at the Christmas dinner table. We know what kind of world we want to live in, and at Christmas, at least, we try to make it happen.

Dr Jacqui Lewis talks about midwifing a better world, and I think Mary knew all about that as she sang the Magnificat. She understood that in birthing her son, she was also participating in the birth of a new world. The words she sang were not the submissive acceptance of a peace-keeper, but the subversive, dangerous prophecy of a peace-maker. Her son, the Prince of Peace, would echo these words, when he quoted the prophet Isaiah at the beginning of his public ministry (Luke 4:14-20). Like his mother before him, he would not keep quiet in order to support and maintain the current state of affairs, but would challenge injustice and turn the world upside down. It would very bad news for the rich and the proud, but very good news for the weak and the vulnerable.

So the invitation of Advent is peace. It's the invitation to quiet our souls and listen for the still, small voice that calls us beloved. It's the invitation to take a rest from the culture that constantly tells us we need more. It's the invitation to leave behind fear and take up trust. It's the invitation to treat ourselves and others with gentleness. The Prince of Peace himself invites us to participate with him in midwifing a better world.

The good news is, we're already doing it. Glimpses of light are breaking through as we feed the homeless, give to those in need and comfort those who are lonely. Advent invites us to take a long-term view of peace, continuing to work for the good of the whole world, one person at a time, long after the celebrations of Christmas have ended.

Reflection

Which aspects of peace have most captured your attention this week?

How might you continue to serve those in need after Christmas is over?

Breath prayer

Inhale: We work towards peace

Exhale: That everyone might flourish.

WEEK 3

Joy

DAY 13

Start Small

Psalm 30:5

Weeping may remain for the night,
but joy comes in the morning.

Psalm 34:8

Taste and see that the Lord is good.

Sometimes joy feels like it's just beyond our grasp. We'd like to feel happy and content, but we're still waiting for our longed-for breakthrough, big achievement or special occasion. We'd like to feel pleasure and delight, but with so much grief and suffering in the world, joy can feel out of reach or even inappropriate in the face of other people's pain.

But I think joy is both closer and more important than it seems. Joy was never meant to invalidate sorrow, but to help us carry it with lightness and grace. Joy adds depth and delight to our days. It helps us move through the world with a little more ease and comfort. Joy reminds us that despair doesn't have to have the last word.

Joy doesn't just come to us in the big, Christmas morning occasions, but can be found nestling among the ordinary, everyday moments of life. I like to think about the shepherds in the nativity story sitting around their fire, appreciating its warmth and crackle, comforted by the sleepy bleating of their sheep, happily tired from a day's work well done. They got their big moment when the angels appeared, but right before that, there were joys to be found in the small, unseen moments too.

Advent is a good time to practice leaning into joy. There are so many simple pleasures to savour. The glimmer of lights on a neighbour's Christmas tree, the taste of a delicious, seasonal treat, the sweet harmonies of a familiar carol. If joy feels far away, start small and use your physical senses to notice what feels good, smells divine or sounds amazing. Learning to appreciate each good, true or beautiful thing, no matter how small or fleeting, becomes a trail of breadcrumbs that we can follow into contentment and delight.

I want to follow those breadcrumbs of delight right through Advent and out the other side so I have a practice of joy to sustain me once the festivities of the season are over. I want to appreciate each chocolate from my Advent calendar as it melts on my tongue. I want to sing out loud to Christmas songs on the radio, enjoy finely decorated trees and breathe in the scent of mulled wine and mince pies. I want to practice cultivating delight so I can hold joy in one hand, even while I hold sorrow in the other. Are you with me?

Reflection

How does joy feel for you – easy to come by? Hard to access? Something else?

Which small joys of the Christmas season bring you particular delight?

Breath Prayer

Inhale: You are my joy.

Exhale: I delight in you.

DAY 14

Be Present

Psalm 118:24

This is the day that the Lord has made –
I will rejoice and be glad in it.

Matthew 6:34

Therefore do not worry about tomorrow,
for tomorrow will worry about itself.
Each day has enough trouble of its own.

As you might have realised yesterday, I have had a complicated relationship with joy. Joy can make me feel vulnerable, because what if the thing I'm enjoying goes wrong? What if my future doesn't work out like I wanted it to? What if I feel stupid for celebrating when suffering might be just around the corner? What if a double-decker-sized tragedy ploughs through my life and I'm engulfed by a grief I didn't foresee and wasn't prepared for?

You and I both know that life doesn't always turn out as we'd planned, hoped or dreamed. We know that terrible and painful things do happen, and we can't wish them away. So we steel ourselves against future catastrophe by imagining what could go wrong and grieving in advance, as though it will take the sting out of any pain that comes our way.[iii]

But the problem is, doing this doesn't work. No amount of planning can insulate us from experiencing suffering. That's just part of being a human living in the world. All we're doing by grieving things that may never happen is stealing our own emotional energy and robbing ourselves of enjoying today's delights. If the worst does happen, God himself will lead us tenderly through the valley of our grief. We don't have to walk it alone, in advance.

I'm learning that the best thing we can do is to focus our thoughts on what's going on in this present moment. As our reading for today says, there are probably enough troubles to keep us occupied here without having to borrow any from tomorrow! But the present is full of things to enjoy, too. So I want to stay present in *this* moment, and enjoy *this* day that the Lord has made, with all its opportunities for delight, both big and small.

I've come to believe that joy is a hopeful and brave emotion. It dares to believe that right here and right now there are good and beautiful things worth celebrating. It dares to believe that whatever troubles we might have will not erase those good things. It offers us the gift of knowing that suffering is not the end of our story and that life is still worth living.

So let's take a deep breath together, ground ourselves in the present moment and enjoy the gift of this day that God has given us.

Reflection

Which things that feel joyful can also make you feel vulnerable?

What helps you to stay present in this moment when you are tempted to worry about the future?

Breath prayer

Inhale: This day is your gift to me

Exhale: I will rejoice and be glad in it.

DAY 15

Give Thanks

1 Thessalonians 5:16-18

Rejoice always, pray continually,
give thanks in all circumstances;
for this is God's will for you in Christ Jesus.

Being thankful in all circumstances sometimes feels a bit 'wishy-washy' like we're expected to be Pollyanna playing the glad game, finding tenuous reasons to be thankful for the awful things we experience. I don't think we need to do this. God doesn't inflict suffering on us to teach us to be grateful. Sometimes terrible things just happen and it's okay to be honest about it.

I think gratitude is like a candle in the dark. It doesn't change the contours of the room, but it creates a different atmosphere. It softens hard edges. It offers warmth and sheds a kinder, more gentle light on things. It brings us hope and makes the darkness feel more bearable.

Genuine gratitude helps us step over the threshold between joy and despair. When I'm stuck in the always-and-never-type thinking of hopelessness – *things will **always** be this bad, this will **never** work out* – gratitude recalibrates my heart and my mind and helps me find perspective. It calls me back to the truth that not everything is a terrible disaster. Richard Rohr often says that God comes to us disguised as our life. When I view my life through the lens of gratitude, I find there is so much to be thankful for. I'm grateful for the air in my lungs and the kindness of my husband. I'm thankful for the tree at the bottom of my garden and the birds who come to play in our bird bath. I'm thankful for friends and flowers and books and hot showers. The list goes on and on. Life does not wholly consist of tragedy and when I choose to cultivate gratitude I'm able to lay worry and fear aside and find joy in the present moment.

Gratitude helps us to lift our gaze and remember that we belong to a bigger story. It's the story we are telling again this Advent, of a baby King born in a stable, the God of the universe come to earth as a helpless human, the God who came to be with us so we never have to face anything alone again. Gratitude helps us to remember that all of life is a gift, sustained by grace. It doesn't all depend on us to be perfect or get everything right. We don't have to foresee our own future, erase our own past or control our own present. We can kneel once again with gratitude before the manger, resting our hearts in the goodness and kindness of God.

Reflection

What helps you to cultivate a thankful attitude?

What are you grateful for today?

Breath Prayer

Inhale: Thank you

Exhale: Thank you.

DAY 16

Use Your Imagination

Ephesians 3:18-19

I pray that the eyes of your heart may be enlightened in order that you may know the hope to which he has called you, the riches of his glorious inheritance in his holy people, and his incomparably great power for us who believe.

Over the last few years I have become slightly obsessed with watching house renovation shows on T.V. I love watching the transformation from something that's old, dirty and outdated into a beautiful, functional home a family can enjoy. It always strikes me how much imagination these projects require. Homeowners have to be realistic about what they're dealing with, but must also be able to see the potential in their property. Their vision for what their home could be like is what helps them keep going when they hit the inevitable obstacles and problems they encounter along the way.

C. S. Lewis famously described God's work in our lives as a renovation project: we think God is there to redecorate a few rooms and fix the leak in the roof, but it turns out God has plans to create something much grander – a palace he comes to inhabit himself. I think that's because God sees all our potential and possibility. He both loves us exactly as we are now, in our run-down, broken state, and knows all that we can become as we learn to embrace the truth of our belovedness.

When we pray, along with the Apostle Paul, that the eyes of our hearts might be enlightened, what we're asking for is holy imagination – the ability to see all that God has for us and all that he's calling us into. It brings us joy and hope to recognise that we're not stuck with the way things are. We're not trapped in our current habits, thoughts or situations. Holy imagination helps us to see there's a different way and inspires us to change.

Divine imagination also helps us to see that our world is not as stuck as we thought it might be, either. In his book *The Way of Imagination* Scott Russell Sanders points out that every major societal change occurred because someone could imagine a better way. Someone imagined a better way than slavery, a better way than denying women the vote, a better way than child labour. It's a joyful practice to imagine how much better our world can be. Imagine a world with no violence or poverty. Imagine a world where racism and misogyny no longer exist. Imagine a world where everyone has access to clean water and nourishing food. Imagine a world where trauma is healed and every person knows they are loved. If we can imagine something, we can begin taking steps towards it. Big changes don't happen easily or overnight, but the joy we are growing in now will sustain us between the reality of our world as it is, and the realisation of our bold, bright, beautiful vision for the world as it could be.

Reflection

Are there any ways that imagination can help you feel less stuck in your life?

How can you imagine our world as a better place? What part do you think you have to play in making that a reality?

Breath prayer

Inhale: God, open my eyes

Exhale: Show me what you see.

DAY 17

Seek Treasure

Matthew 6:19-21

Do not store up for yourselves treasures on earth, where moths and vermin destroy, and where thieves break in and steal. But store up for yourselves treasures in heaven, where moths and vermin do not destroy, and where thieves do not break in and steal. For where your treasure is, there your heart will be also.

Matthew 13:44

The kingdom of heaven is like treasure hidden in a field. When a man found it, he hid it again, and then in his joy went and sold all he had and bought that field.

Western culture has a lot to say about what human flourishing might look like. Being successful is mostly equated with money, power and influence. We're supposed to amass wealth for ourselves so we can live in fancy houses and go on luxury holidays. We're meant to be highly successful in our chosen careers so we attain prestige and authority. We're supposed to be thin and beautiful with the perfect family and friends so everyone wants to be like us. This is what our society upholds and celebrates as its virtues. These are the kinds of people we respect and desire to emulate.

However, if you're anything like me, it's not the glaringly obvious pitfalls of fame and fortune that trip you up, but the more subtle ones. I'm not seeking the wealth of a lottery winner, but I can feel discontentment creep in when I visit a friend who has a nicer house than mine. I'm not running after the fame of a movie star, but I do get a bit more of my self-worth from likes and comments on social media than perhaps I should. I'm grateful for my family and friends, but I'm sometimes envious of people who seem to be more popular than me. I don't expect to have a career as a super model, but I do often feel dissatisfied with, and critical of, my appearance.

In those situations I have often found comfort in the words of Mother Teresa, who said that we are not called to be successful, we are called to be faithful. In many ways, that comes as a relief! It helps me to remember to let go of comparison. It helps me to stop struggling after things that will never fully satisfy me. It reminds me that I'm called to be faithful with what God has put in my hands and the measure of influence he has given me, and that that is enough.

In Philippians 2, we are reminded that Jesus humbled himself, even to death on a cross, because he was fully secure in his identity as God's beloved child. He didn't need other things or people to affirm his self-worth or to bring him reassurance. He was so secure in who he was that he was able to leave the riches of heaven behind and come to earth as a helpless, dependent baby.

Advent is a good season to re-examine our priorities and consider where our true treasure lies. As we take up Mother Teresa's call to be faithful, and Jesus' example of humility, one small step at a time, we will find a deep, abiding joy that anchors us throughout the ups and downs of life, and can never be taken away.

Reflection

Where might you be prone to seeking joy from the world's idea of success?

How does the idea of being faithful, rather than successful, make you feel?

Breath prayer

Inhale: You are my treasure

Exhale: I find my joy in you.

DAY 18

Come Home

John 14:23

Jesus replied, "Anyone who loves me will obey my teaching. My Father will love them, and we will come to them and make our home with them."

Luke 15:20-24

"But while he was still a long way off, his father saw him and was filled with compassion for him; he ran to his son, threw his arms around him and kissed him.

"The son said to him, 'Father, I have sinned against heaven and against you. I am no longer worthy to be called your son.'

"But the father said to his servants, 'Quick! Bring the best robe and put it on him. Put a ring on his finger and sandals on his feet. Bring the fattened calf and kill it. Let's have a feast and celebrate. For this son of mine was dead and is alive again; he was lost and is found.' So they began to celebrate."

Thoughts of home seem particularly poignant at this time of year. We make plans to spend time with family and friends, and mourn the absence of those we can't be with. I get nostalgic listening to Chris Rea's *Driving Home for Christmas*, conjuring up memories of perfect childhood Christmases in a family home my parents moved out of years ago.

But home is much more than a house. Home is a place of acceptance. A place where you can be fully known and fully loved. It's that place where you're not just tolerated, but actively wanted and delighted in. It's a place that holds your memories and your heart; a place where your needs are met and you feel welcomed and secure. Home is where you belong, the place where you can find fullness of joy.

At the heart of the Gospel is the invitation to come home. In Luke's Gospel, Jesus tells three parables about three lost things all in a row: the lost sheep, the lost coin and the lost son. What strikes me about them is the joy of the finder in every story. The shepherd celebrates finding his sheep, the woman rejoices at finding her coin, the father throws a party in honour of his son coming home. These parables offer us a picture of a God who doesn't just tolerate us, but actively seeks us out, offers us a deep sense of security and belonging in him, and takes great delight in us. When we retell the Christmas story, we're remembering the Good Shepherd who came to earth to find each one of us and bring us home to God the Father. We remember that nothing, not even death, can separate us from the love of God, who welcomes us to himself with great tenderness and affection. We're remembering how much God celebrates when one of his children comes home to him.

So the invitation of Advent is joy. It's the invitation to come home to God and find out how much he delights in you. It's an invitation to participate in the small, everyday joys that come our way. It's an invitation to live in the present moment and find gratitude for what is right in front of us. It's the invitation to use our imagination and see what could be possible, and to fix our eyes on Jesus, the true source of all our joy.

If you're feeling lost among the chaos and preparations of the season, or if you're not quite sure where home is, may you know today that you are seen and known, loved and wanted, delighted in and rejoiced over. May you know that God makes his home in you, as you make your home in him.

Reflection

What images, thoughts or feelings does the idea of 'home' bring up for you?

Which aspects of joy have most captured your attention this week?

Breath Prayer

Inhale: I am at home in you

Exhale: As you are at home in me.

WEEK 4

Love

DAY 19

Make Room

Luke 2:16-19

So [the shepherds] hurried off and found Mary and Joseph, and the baby, who was lying in the manger. When they had seen him, they spread the word concerning what had been told them about this child, and all who heard it were amazed at what the shepherds said to them. But Mary treasured up all these things and pondered them in her heart.

The stories of Christmas are famous for how they ask people to make room for Jesus. The inn keeper is asked to find Mary and Joseph a place to stay. Joseph is asked to make room for someone else's child, and Mary of course, is asked to make space for Jesus to gestate and grow inside her. Mary not only held space in her womb, but also in her heart. She treasured the precious words about her son, considering all the prophecies and promises that were made about him.

Advent gives us the chance to consider what God might want to conceive and bring to birth within each of us. This in-between time, when we're waiting for the Saviour to come again, gives us space to process our emotions, give voice to our fears, our anxieties and our dreams. It's a time when we might anticipate what is to come, remind ourselves of what God has promised and let hope, peace, joy and love grow in us again, knowing that the Holy Spirit always leads us towards wholeness and flourishing.

As we make room for God, we find that God is also making room for us. In the Bible, the word we translate as compassion comes from the Hebrew word for womb. We are held with compassion and tenderness by the God who nurtures us and makes room for us to grow, just as a mother holds a tender, safe space for her baby. There is room for us in God's heart and at God's table and we are loved just as we are.

Making room is also a beautiful gift we can offer each other in this season of giving. Mary not only made room for the joy of Jesus's birth, but also the pain that came with it, and the pain she would again experience at his death. When we make room to hear each other's experiences and validate each other's feelings – both the good and the messy and difficult – we create a safe space. We create a space for deepening friendship, ongoing healing and a community rooted in love.

I wonder who you might make room for this Advent? I wonder who is making room for you?

Reflection

How does it feel to know that God is making room for you?

Are there people in your life who might need you to make room for them?

Breath Prayer

Inhale: I make room for you God

Exhale: As you make room for me.

DAY 20

Follow the Star

Matthew 2:1-8

After Jesus was born in Bethlehem in Judea, during the time of King Herod, Magi from the east came to Jerusalem and asked, "Where is the one who has been born king of the Jews? We saw his star when it rose and have come to worship him."

When King Herod heard this he was disturbed, and all Jerusalem with him. When he had called together all the people's chief priests and teachers of the law, he asked them where the Messiah was to be born. "In Bethlehem in Judea," they replied, "for this is what the prophet has written:

"'But you, Bethlehem, in the land of Judah,
are by no means least among the rulers of Judah;
for out of you will come a ruler
who will shepherd my people Israel.'"

Then Herod called the Magi secretly and found out from them the exact time the star had appeared. He sent them to Bethlehem and said, "Go and search carefully for the child. As soon as you find him, report to me, so that I too may go and worship him."

Starlight flickers and glimmers in the dark, small pinpoints of light gracing the night sky. It takes the light from one of our nearest stars, Sirius, around four years to reach the earth. Starlight from further distances can take thousands of years. It's quite a journey.

We're not supposed to be thinking about the Magi until after Christmas. After all, they don't appear in the nativity story until after Jesus is born and the church traditionally celebrates their arrival in January, at the festival of Epiphany. But I like to think about the journey they took before they reached Bethlehem. How far did they travel? How did they know which star to follow? Did they ever doubt they would make it? How did they keep going? The Wise Men needed wisdom and discernment to follow the star and move away from Herod. They needed faith and hope to follow the light and move towards Jesus. Perhaps that is why they chose to travel in community. "If one falls down," so the bible says, "the other can pick him up" (Ecclesiastes 4:9).

I wonder how you feel about your own journey this Advent? Perhaps you feel certain and steadfast about where you're going, or perhaps you're feeling lost and unsure. Maybe you have a clear sense of purpose and direction, or maybe the skies are cloudy where you are, and you can't see the way forward. Either way, I hope you know that you're not alone. I hope you find companionship and encouragement to sustain you when you need it most. I hope you find safe people to help you discern the way forward and walk with you on your journey. I hope you come to know the God of love, who will never leave or abandon you, in a new and deeper way this Christmas season.

The Wise Men trusted that love would lead them to the stable to find Jesus, our bright Morning Star, who will one day banish all our 'night-time' experiences for good. As you look up at the night sky this evening, may you know that you have been in God's heart for as long as the stars have existed and may you know, deep inside, that you are being led by love too.

Reflection

Think about the journey of your life. How does it feel at the moment? Exciting? Confusing? Scary? Bring those feelings before God and ask him to be with you.

Who is accompanying you on your journey? If you're feeling alone, how might you find safe community?

Breath Prayer

Inhale: I trust your love

Exhale: To show me the way.

DAY 21

Good Gifts

Matthew 2:9-12

After they had heard the king, they went on their way, and the star they had seen when it rose went ahead of them until it stopped over the place where the child was. When they saw the star, they were overjoyed. On coming to the house, they saw the child with his mother Mary, and they bowed down and worshiped him. Then they opened their treasures and presented him with gifts of gold, frankincense and myrrh. And having been warned in a dream not to go back to Herod, they returned to their country by another route.

I love the part of the Christmas story we find in our reading today. I find the joy of the Magi, as they finally meet Jesus, to be infectious. I'm captured by how they truly recognise who Jesus is, even as a baby. I'm heartened by their love, honour and worship for him. I love how they unpack their treasures to give to the One, True Treasure they have been seeking for all this time.

According to church tradition, the gifts the Magi gave to Jesus were especially chosen for their significance. Gold denotes his status as a king, frankincense is a symbol of his priestly role, advocating for the people, and myrrh prefigures the burial spices that would be used at his death.

This time of year we also choose gifts based on what we know about the recipient. What do they want? What do they need? What might they enjoy? What might be meaningful or special to them? It's a way of demonstrating care for those we love. It's way of investing in someone. It's a way of showing someone that we know them and have spent time thinking about them.

But have you ever stopped to consider that, just as Jesus is God's gift to the world, so are you? Perhaps your empathy and compassion are exactly what someone else needs right now. Perhaps your particular brand of humour and your fun-loving nature are just what someone else would enjoy. Maybe the way you smile or the way you give big bear hugs would be really meaningful to someone. Perhaps the way you let a friend sit in your kitchen when they feel lonely is the best gift they could receive.

The beautiful thing about being God's gift to the world is that you don't have to be any different than you already are. You don't need to have special skills or talents. You don't have to have the perfect home, or family, or life. You don't need to change at all. You just need to show up as yourself and be open to who might need you, just as you are.

In this season of gift-giving, I pray you would know that you are both wanted and needed. Your presence here on earth is a gift from God and a sign of his kindness to us all.

Reflection

How does it feel to think of yourself as a gift from God to others?

Who might appreciate your presence, rather than a gift, this Christmas?

Breath Prayer

Inhale: Jesus, you are my greatest gift

Exhale: As I am a gift to your world.

DAY 22

Tender Mercy

Luke 1:76-79

"And you, my child, will be called a prophet
of the Most High;
for you will go on before the Lord to
prepare the way for him,
to give his people the knowledge of salvation
through the forgiveness of their sins,
because of the tender mercy of our God,
by which the rising sun will come to us from heaven
to shine on those living in darkness
and in the shadow of death,
to guide our feet into the path of peace."

Before the birth of Jesus, God's people were waiting for a Messiah. They had been subjugated by the cruel, oppressive Roman regime for a long time and were expecting the promised Saviour to rescue them. They wanted a warrior-king who would slay their enemies and lead them to a triumphant and decisive political victory.

If we're honest, this kind of Messiah is sometimes what we'd like, too. We might not want Jesus to actually slay our enemies, but we would like to conquer them in some way. We want a Messiah who will justify our point of view and take our side. We want some assurances that 'our' opinions are right, while 'their' opinions are wrong. We want a Saviour to help us win the moral victory and take down those who disagree with us, if not with an actual sword, at least with a well-timed, viral tweet.

But God's salvation did not come through punishment and domination. It came through Jesus: servant and king, carpenter's son and Saviour, ordinary man and miracle worker, human son of Mary and divine Son of God.

Following the way of Jesus means laying down the 'either/or' thinking of taking sides, and embracing the 'both/and' thinking of compassion and reconciliation instead. It means learning to recognise that I am a mixture of good *and* bad and that the bad in me does not cancel out the good. It means I can recognise my own strengths *and* weaknesses while knowing that I am fully loved and accepted as God's child. When I can see this in myself, I can begin to recognise it in others, too. I can see that we are all a mixture of good and bad, gifts and flaws, shadow and light.[iv]

Maturity is learning that there is no 'us and them', only 'us' as Father Greg Boyle would say.[v] God's tender mercy and loving kindness help me find grace for those with whom I disagree. They help me understand that life is not always black and white but mostly comes in shades of grey. They help me remember that I am in need of forgiveness and mercy just as much as anyone else. The tender mercy of God draws me towards empathy and kindness and away from judgement and shame.

In Jesus, all creation has been reconciled to God (Col. 1:19-20), and we are his disciples when we participate in that ongoing reconciliation within ourselves, between each other and with the whole earth. We do this with full assurance that God is love, and love never, ever fails.

Reflection

In what ways have you been prone to 'either/or' thinking?

How might God's tender mercy draw you away from shame and towards empathy, both for yourself and others?

Breath Prayer

Inhale: Draw me towards empathy and kindness

Exhale: Lead me away from judgement and shame.

DAY 23

Stay Curious

Matthew 18:2-4

He called a little child to him, and placed the child among them. And he said: "Truly I tell you, unless you change and become like little children, you will never enter the kingdom of heaven. Therefore, whoever takes the lowly position of this child is the greatest in the kingdom of heaven."

John 3:1-3

Now there was a Pharisee, a man named Nicodemus who was a member of the Jewish ruling council. He came to Jesus at night and said, "Rabbi, we know that you are a teacher who has come from God. For no one could perform the signs you are doing if God were not with him."

Jesus replied, "Very truly I tell you, no one can see the kingdom of God unless they are born again."

Have you ever noticed how Christmas looks through the eyes of a child? It's full of sparkling wonder, hopeful expectation and great excitement. I love watching the innocent delight of my nieces and nephews who still believe in the magic of it all. They're not too embarrassed to enter whole-heartedly into the spirit of celebration and they have no shame in asking for exactly what they want. Children spend the days of Advent in a state of joyful anticipation, hardly able to wait for all the good food, good gifts and good fun they know are coming their way.

In our Bible reading today, Jesus said if we want to become part of his kingdom of love, we must learn to become like little children. But what might that mean? If you know any children, you know they are as likely to fight and argue as adults! But children have no social capital – no power, money or authority to wield or defend. They don't hide their desires or motives. They have not yet learned to be cynical or insincere.

What children do have is boundless curiosity. If you've ever spent time with a three-year-old you'll know about their incessant questioning, where every answer you give is followed by *"but why?!"* Children view the world with fresh eyes. Everything is new and interesting to them. They are unencumbered by the need to perform and impress, but want to soak in everything they can about this exciting, wonder-filled world they are encountering for the first time.

We become like children when we suspend our disenchantment, lay aside our cynicism and cultivate curiosity about the world and the people around us.

Learning to ask questions helps us to move away from shame and judgement towards ourselves and others, and lean into empathy instead. *"I wonder why that person reacted so badly?"* we can learn to ask. *"I wonder what hurt or fear they are feeling?"* Or *"I wonder why **I** reacted so badly? I wonder what shame or pain **I'm** feeling right now?"*

Perhaps this is what Jesus meant when he told Nicodemus he must be born again to enter God's kingdom. Perhaps in being born as a child himself, Jesus was modelling for us the need to recover a child-like sense of awe, wonder and curiosity. Perhaps he was inviting us to recognise that we are all God's children, in need of kindness and understanding.

Charles Dickens wrote that 'it is good to be children sometimes, and never better than at Christmas, when its mighty Founder was a child himself.' What better place to rediscover our child-like wonder and curiosity than marvelling again at the mystery of Jesus' birth?

Reflection

How might curiosity help you stay out of shaming yourself or others?

What might you do to recapture some child-like curiosity and wonder today?

Breath Prayer

Inhale: Help me see again

Exhale: through the eyes of a child.

DAY 24

God With Us

Isaiah 7:14

Therefore the Lord himself will give you a sign:
the virgin will conceive and give birth to a son
and she will call him Immanuel.

Matthew 1:20-23

"Joseph son of David, do not be afraid to take Mary home
as your wife, because what is conceived in her is from the
Holy Spirit. She will give birth to a son, and you are to
give him the name Jesus, because he will save his people
from their sins."

All this took place to fulfil what the Lord had said
through the prophet: "The virgin will conceive and give
birth to a son, and they will call him Immanuel" (which
means "God with us").

The waiting nears its end and the anticipation heightens. We come at last to the moment of holy mystery; we arrive at the threshold of all we have been hoping for: Immanuel – God come to be *with* us. Mary and the Spirit labour together as Jesus is born. Pain and joy, tearing open and tenderness, sweat and delight, blood and water thrust the Son of God into the world he created. The heavenly hosts burst into song at the glory and wonder of it all.

For God so loved the world, that he sent his only son to be with us in ways we can touch, taste, hear, see and smell. Our God comes to us in flesh and blood, skin and bone, muscle and memory – eternity laid in a manger. This is not a far off deity, abandoning us to our fate, but a God who stays near in the messy and the mundane, the delight and the sorrow, the anxiety and the unknown, the brokenness and the healing and everything else it means to be human. He knows what it's like because he's been here and lived as one of us. And he's still inviting us to experience his presence now, in the bread and the wine; in the water that baptises and sustains us; in the candles we light and the air we inhale; in the kindness of family and friends. All creation points us towards the love of the Saviour who can't take his eyes off us, who can't stay away from the ones he so dearly loves.

So the invitation of Advent is to live as God's beloved children. It's an invitation to participate in reconciliation, moving towards empathy and kindness and away from judgement and shame. It's an invitation to make room for

God, knowing that he is making room for us. It's an invitation to recognise that God has good gifts for us and that we are also his gift to the world. It's an invitation to recognise that we are led by love to find the Light of the World, the One who will never abandon or reject us, the One who will stay close when everyone else is gone, the One who left heaven and laid down his life so that we never have to live without him again.

Reflection

Which aspect of love has resonated most deeply with you this week?

How might you find God's presence in concrete and specific ways?

Breath Prayer

Inhale: Immanuel

Exhale: God is with us.

A BLESSING

As our time together draws to a close, I would like to offer you a blessing and a prayer, that God's presence would be evident with you, long after the festivities of this season are over.

May you find hope that runs deeper than your despair,
and is stronger than your pain.
May you find hope that pays attention to your sorrow,
but refuses to be overcome by the dark.

May you find peace that calms your anxieties,
and soothes your fears.
May you find peace that stills your soul,
and calls you to work towards the flourishing of all people.

May you find joy that sustains you in sadness,
and causes you to notice beauty and goodness
wherever you go.
May you find joy that takes delight in the small things,
and opens your imagination to astounding possibilities,

May you fully experience the all-encompassing love of God
that heals your heart and stays present with you always.
May you know the love of God that is deeper
than you could have hoped for,
Wider and more inclusive than you could have asked for,
And beyond anything you could have imagined
in your wildest dreams.

Amen

ACKNOWLEDGEMENTS

I'm so thankful to everyone who has encouraged and supported my writing, especially my friends, social media friends and readers. These words are for you, and I hope you find in them tenderness and compassion. I hope they remind you that you're loved.

Particular thanks go to:

My 'writing posse' – Liz Carter, Claire Musters and Lucy Rycroft – thank you for praying, answering questions, believing in me and being a much-valued source of expertise and encouragement. I'm so thankful for each one of you. Special thanks to Liz for your formatting and editing skills as well as your beautiful cover design and walking me through how to self-publish.

Aundi Kolber and Marlena Graves – your kindness, friendship and belief in me have meant so much – thank you.

Christiana Peterson, Steve Wiens, Jonathan Puddle, Ruth Leigh, Liz Carter and Claire Musters – thank you for your kind words and your willingness to support my work.

Mum and Dad – thank you for always supporting and believing in me.

My husband, Tim – none of this would have been possible without you. I'm grateful for the care, comfort, support and love you show me in so many ways, every single day. You will always and forever be my favourite.

ABOUT THE AUTHOR

Abby Ball is a teacher, writer and avid reader. When she's not in the classroom helping to shape young minds, she spends her time shaping words on the page, writing towards hope in the transitions between where we are and where we want to be. Abby lives with her husband, Tim and their cat, Otta.

abbyball.substack.com

ENDNOTES

[i] With thanks to Shauna Neiquist for pointing this out in her book *Present Over Perfect*, Grand Rapids: Zondervan, 2016.

[ii] I am indebted to Henri Nouwen for this insight, from his book *Life of the Beloved,* London: Hodder and Stoughton, 2016.

[iii] Brené Brown calls this 'foreboding joy' and you can read more about it in her book, *Daring Greatly,* London: Penguin Life, 2012.

[iv] With thanks to Richard Rohr, whose thinking informed my own here: https://cac.org/daily-meditations/a-change-of-consciousness-2022-09-13/ accessed 14/09/2022

[v] You can read more about this in Greg Boyle's book, *Tattoos on the Heart: The Power of Boundless Compassion,* New York: Free Press, 2011.